# The Quest:

## The Path to Dog Training Success

***Mindset Before Methods***

***Dennis Hayre***

ISBN 978-0-7414-9683-6 Paperback
ISBN 978-0-7414-9684-3 eBook
ISBN 978-0-7414-9685-0 Audiobook
Library of Congress Control Number: 2013913281

Printed in the United States of America

Published July 2013

INFINITY PUBLISHING
1094 New DeHaven Street, Suite 100
West Conshohocken, PA 19428-2713
Toll-free (877) BUY BOOK
Local Phone (610) 941-9999
Fax (610) 941-9959
Info@buybooksontheweb.com
www.buybooksontheweb.com

# Table of Contents

**Introduction** .................... **1**

**1. The Beginning of It All** .................... **3**

**2. Meeting My Mentor–The Interview** .................... **6**

**3. Mindset Before Methods** .................... **12**

**4. Principle One: Leadership** .................... **16**

*Leadership Checklist* .................... 24

**5. Principle Two: State of Mind – The Key to Responsible and Successful Dog Training** .................... **26**

*State of Mind Checklist* .................... 39

**6. Principle Three: Confidence** .................... **41**

*Confidence Checklist* .................... 51

**7. Principle Four: Productivity** .................... **52**

*Productivity Checklist* .................... 58

**8. Principle Five: The Compound Effect ............................59**

*Compound Effect Checklist* ....................................................66

**9. Principle Six: Equilibrium ................................................67**

*Equilibrium Checklist* ..............................................................72

**10. One Last Thing: Be Careful of What You Become in Pursuit of What You Want ..........................73**

**11. Conclusion ....................................................................81**

# The Quest:

## The Path to Dog Training Success

***Mindset Before Methods***

# Introduction

Training dogs is truly my passion. I have been a student of dog training for many years and have had the opportunity to learn from several great trainers, some directly and some indirectly through observation and study. Having studied numerous training methods and training philosophies, I believe that the proper training mindset is more important than the choice of method. Different people using the same methods get varying results. If the variation resulted from the methods, then those using these same methods would get similar results. Thus, the difference in training outcomes stems from how those methods are applied, rather than the actual methods themselves. Though I focus on retriever training, this principle of mindset being more important than methods applies to any form of dog training. In fact, it applies to all sports and to life in general.

This book is not about training methods, but rather about the importance of having the proper mindset before beginning to apply any given method. This is why the principles are applicable to all forms of dog training and dog sports. I wrote this book in the form of a fable to make the principles more interesting and accessible.

I have spent the last twenty years developing a training program that produces good results for hunting dogs, hunt test dogs, field trial dogs, and family dogs in a manner that focuses on cultivating a positive working attitude in dog and handler. I wholeheartedly believe that to produce results at the expense of the dog's well-being or psyche is a total failure. And to produce good results with certain types of dogs while destroying the psyche of other types of dogs is also an absolute failure.

As a lifelong student of dogs and the training process, I am still learning and evolving as a trainer and handler; I still make more mistakes than I would like. I hope this book will help all of us become better mentors to our dogs and better stewards of our great dog sports.

Dennis Hayre
Sutter Creek, CA
2013

# CHAPTER ONE

## *The Beginning of It All*

It all began when I stumbled upon a local retriever field trial.[1] I was mesmerized by what I saw those dogs do. At that moment, I knew I wanted to become a dog trainer and train dogs to those same incredible levels.

My then six-month-old lab became my first trainee. Full of enthusiasm, I joined my local retriever club and bought every book and video I could find on dog training and training retrievers. Seeing up close what these dogs could do fueled my fascination, and I became totally intrigued by the training process. I had a burning desire to learn as much as I could as fast as I could, even if it meant losing sleep.

After a few training sessions with my dog, I realized that training did not always go as easily and as smoothly

---

[1] Field trial: An event where dogs compete against one another in situations that test their natural and trained abilities. In this case, retriever field trials are based on retrieving on land and water. These trials are comprised of advanced retrieving tasks that take an incredible amount of desire, ability, and trainability. What these events ask of these dogs goes way beyond what a hunting dog would need to do.

as the videos made it look. I concluded that either I had a really dumb dog or I was totally missing something. Granted, I was new to the training process, but I still felt things should have been going better than they were. I could not find solutions for when my dog responded differently from how the books said he should. Frustrated by my lack of progress, I became more committed than ever to learn how to train a retriever.

In an effort to get some answers, I found a local trainer who was willing to work with me. Excited to start the process and willing to pay almost any price to learn how to do this right, I arranged my schedule so I could work with the pro five days a week. But after about two weeks of training, I realized that something was amiss. I was following all of the trainer's instructions, but I began to feel uncomfortable doing some of things he suggested. He was asking me to apply a lot of pressure to my dog. When I questioned the trainer, he said that such pressure was a necessary part of training retrievers to high levels. Intuitively, it just felt wrong. So, disappointed and frustrated, I decided to end my lessons with this trainer. At the time, I didn't realize how my well my instincts had served me. I have since found that many new people experience that same thing, and not all of them are able to get out of the situation before serious damage is done to their dogs.

Undeterred, I began my quest to find a top trainer who not only produced great results but whose training methods I could live with. After much research, I felt I had found the right person. The question was whether he would agree to
work with me.

# CHAPTER TWO

## *Meeting My Mentor – The Interview*

Jim Hill, in the opinion of many, was the top field trial retriever trainer in the country. He had won several National Championships and was renown for producing great dogs with happy attitudes from dogs of all types of temperaments. I had been trying for almost a year, via phone calls and emails, to set up an appointment with Mr. Hill.

One fall evening, the phone rang as I was coming inside from dog training. I answered the phone, and a brusque yet warm voice on the other end said, "This is Jim Hill, is Jack Blakely in?"

"This is Jack," I replied.

"Jack Blakely, you are an extremely persistent man." He went on to say, "I have received all your emails and phone messages, so I know your story. Your desire to learn about dog training intrigued me. If you are willing to take a trip to beautiful Vermont, I would like to speak with you in person. Though, I want to forewarn you – I am not guaranteeing anything as far as working with you. I know you live in California, but if you can be here within a week's time, I will be available."

I made flight, hotel, and rental car reservations as soon as I got off the phone and was on the plane the very next day.

I had a day in Vermont before my meeting with Jim Hill, so I thought I would drive around and enjoy the scenery. I had never experienced autumn in this part of the country. Eye-popping colors saturated the countryside. I took it all in. It absolutely amazed me.

That night, as I looked over my directions to Jim Hill's farm and training area, I began to feel both excited and nervous about our meeting. As I prepared for our meeting, I wondered what kind of questions he would ask and how I would answer them – I didn't want to mess up my opportunity to learn from the great Jim Hill. I knew the only thing I could do was be totally honest and sincere and then let the chips fall where they may. When I fell off to sleep, I did so with the feeling that things would work out just as they should. I slept deeply and woke up feeling refreshed, inspired, and excited for what lay ahead.

*****

As I drove up Jim Hill's long, winding driveway, the beauty of the Vermont countryside once again amazed me. The trees lining the driveway expressed this splendor to the fullest. Within a hundred yards of the house, the road straightened, and a large, two-story house surrounded by exquisite landscaping came into full view. But beyond the beauty of this home, what moved me was the serenity and peace that seemed to surround it all.

I pulled into the circular drive, stepped out of my rental car, and proceed up a few steps to the porch. I felt nervous, but I stood at the door for a just a few moments and looked around once more to absorb the scenery. Then I rapped the brass door knocker.

After a few seconds, a man in his mid-fifties, with a look in his eyes that showed extreme confidence, yet deep humility, opened the door. I immediately felt comfortable; not so much because I was all that self-assured, but because of the ease he exuded.

"You must be Jack Blakely." He smiled and gave me a firm yet not overly aggressive handshake. "Welcome to our home. Come on in – I was just finishing my morning coffee." As he guided me through the entryway into his kitchen, his wife, Cindy, greeted me with a warm smile.

"Would you like a cup of hot Vermont coffee?" she asked. I couldn't resist the invitation, and as I took a sip of the coffee, I thought to myself that this was the first time I had ever had coffee that tasted as good as it smelled.

"I'll leave you boys to yourselves," Cindy said cheerfully. "If you want any more coffee, just help yourself. I am going to be out in the barn checking on our new litter of pups." She then turned and headed out the back porch.

There was a sense of tranquility and warmth to the Hills and their lovely home. I had never felt so relaxed with people I had just met. Yet, while Jim Hill's demeanor put me at ease, I still felt nervous because there was no guarantee that he would accept me as a student.

"Have a seat. We have some things to talk about," Jim said, motioning towards the kitchen table. Not wasting any time, he looked right into my eyes and asked, "What are your reasons for wanting to get into dog training? And what are your reasons for wanting to learn from me?" I took a deep breath and told my story.

*****

Feeling that I had been rambling for some time, which would not have been unusual for me, I paused for a moment. Jim Hill smiled. "I'm impressed with your perception. Indeed, it is possible to produce what you call 'results' in this sport, and in any sport for that matter, by using questionable methods, or, maybe more accurately, by applying methods in a questionable way. To produce so-called 'good results' at the expense of the dog's well-being is not success, no matter how many ribbons and trophies one accumulates. In fact, I would consider it failure."

Jim Hill took a sip of coffee. "If you had a chance to win a National Championship with a dog by using what we both now agree are questionable methods, or questionable application of methods, and if this was the only way to achieve this, would you do it?" He stared penetratingly into my eyes. I knew he would know immediately whether my answer was sincere.

"I would not."

He continued to hold my gaze for several more seconds. "One of the reasons I wanted to meet you in person was because it would allow me to spend some time with you and get a feel for what you are all about. That's difficult to do over the phone or via email." He took another sip of coffee. "If you are still interested, I am willing to teach you the art of dog training."

I grinned. "When can we start?"

Jim Hill stood up, reached out his hand, and smiled warmly. "We will start tomorrow morning, bright and early. Can you be here at six a.m.?"

"No problem," I replied.

Before we parted, Jim Hill added, "I want to make it clear that how I teach may be different from what you're accustomed to, so be open to the unexpected."

I said okay, but on the drive back to my hotel, I wondered what he meant by “the unexpected.” I could not wait until the next morning.

# CHAPTER THREE

## *Mindset Before Methods*

I pulled into Jim's driveway early the next morning, and I felt like a kid on the first day of school. It was a crisp fall morning, and as I stepped out of the car, I wondered what was in store. I had only gone a few steps when I heard Jim yell from the barn, "Jack, come on over!"

Known as the "barn," the state of the art kennel facility amazed me. Climate controlled and well lit, the barn was immaculate yet cozy. Each dog lived in its own clean, dry, and comfortable kennel run. I later found out that a state-of-the-art coil system heated each kennel's flooring in the cold months and cooled it in the warm months.

"Good morning Jack, glad to see you're on time. There's a hot thermos full of coffee sitting there on the table. Grab a cup off the shelf there and pour yourself some while I finish loading the dogs into the dog truck."

I poured myself a cup of coffee and took a sip. Again, the coffee amazingly tasted as good as it smelled. I yelled over to Jim, "What's the secret to this great tasting coffee?"

He chuckled. "It's a Vermont secret that can't be shared with foreigners."

As I watched Jim finish loading up the dogs, I noticed his rapport with them. They responded to his every movement, and he hardly spoke a word. And they looked so happy. I had watched dogs being loaded into dog trucks before, but with nowhere near the ease and calmness.

Jim walked over to the table to pour himself some more coffee, and once again the aroma got to me. I slid my cup over for a top off, and Jim laughed.

"I guess I'm going to have to get a bigger thermos."

He motioned for me to sit down on a hay bale near the table, and he grabbed another bale for himself. As he sat down, he asked, "Do you remember what I said yesterday? That what and how I'm going to teach you probably won't be what you expected?"

"Yes, and I wondered about it quite a bit last night."

"Well, Jack, I won't keep you waiting. I'm not going to start by teaching you training methods. Instead, I'll begin by teaching you the proper mindset of training, so you will then be able to properly apply the methods.

"I have a foundational saying when it comes to training dogs, though it applies to life in general as well: first seek the proper mindset, and all else will fall into place. So that's where we're going to start. Jack, if you don't get this right, nothing else you do will really matter."

Jim paused to let what he had said sink in.

"That really resonates with me," I said. "It makes total sense. How do we start?"

"Jack, here's what we're going to do. There are six major principles that I'm going to share with you. We'll focus on one each week. Each Monday, we'll start by spending thirty minutes or so discussing the principle, and then I'll have you observe me as I train the dogs. Though you'll see me applying various training methods, our focus will be on the mindset behind the methods.

"The training process will provide many opportunities for you to learn about the nuances of each principle. On the morning of each training day, we'll spend a few minutes going over any questions you may have from the day before, and I'm sure you'll have plenty. Then at the end of the week, we'll sit down and go over what you've learned and all that happened during the week.

"I'd highly recommend you take notes and write down your insights and questions. You'll be getting a lot of information – if you don't write it down, you won't retain it. A mentor of mine once said, 'Don't just try to get through the day, but get from the day.' You can only do this by writing down your thoughts and later reflecting on them."

Feeling unprepared, I sheepishly admitted, "I don't have a journal with me – or even a notepad."

Jim smiled kindly. "I thought that might be the case." He pulled a beautiful, tan, rustic-looking leather journal out of his duffel bag. "This is for you."

"Wow. Thank you. I can't wait to use it."

"You don't have to," replied Jim. "Let's gets started."

# CHAPTER FOUR

## *Principle One: Leadership*

"Leadership is the first principle we're going to cover," began Jim. I opened my journal and started taking notes. He smiled and continued, "Dogs, like kids, crave leadership and the security and stability that come from real leadership. Also, ego has no place in leadership. Anytime people place their egos ahead of the dog's well-being, true leadership cannot exist. We'll talk more about this as we go through the principles, but first let me give you my definition of leadership as it relates to dog training. Leadership is producing results while having the dog's best interest and well-being as the top priority at all times. There's a lot in that definition, so let's unpack it a bit.

"Leadership involves trust and respect. These two go together and must be in balance. On one hand, some people don't have the respect of their dogs, and this severely affects results, especially with dogs of certain temperaments. Some people are afraid that if they discipline their dogs, their dogs won't love them. But the truth is that if they don't discipline their dogs, their dogs won't respect them. This can end up causing all kinds of problems, whether or not people compete with their dogs. I could give example after example of how failing to apply proper discipline is detrimental, not only to the dog's well-being, but to the great results we are all seeking.

"On the other hand, leadership and respect have nothing to do with yelling and screaming or hitting a dog with a whip or crop. Humans are the senior partner in the dog/handler relationship and thus have the responsibility to lead with benevolence.

"Jack, one of my greatest challenges as a trainer is getting the owners of the dogs I train to assume the leadership role. True leadership is a presence, a state of mind. I believe it can be cultivated, though obviously it comes more naturally to some than others.

"There will be plenty of opportunity to go into more detail as we progress. And in reality, all the principles involve, or are a part of, leadership. The take home point here is that while abuse and methods that instill fear clearly are not leadership, neither is allowing the dogs to 'rule the roost' so to speak. But enough talk, Jack; let's see how this relates to actually training the dogs."

*****

Jim took one of the dogs out of its kennel and brought him out near where we had been talking. Jim explained that this was a six-month-old male with a lot of confidence and a mind of his own.

"Jack," Jim asked me, "Are you familiar with the term 'force fetch?'"[2]

"Yes, I think so."

"Then you may know that one purpose of force fetching is to get reliable delivery to hand.[3] Even though some dogs retrieve naturally, we may still have to teach the dog to hold a bumper, and then a bird, properly. This means holding it firmly with no mouthing, chewing, or chomping.

"But a more important purpose of force fetching is to teach the dog how to properly respond to pressure. Applying pressure is unfair unless a dog knows how to turn the pressure off. Thus, to be truly force fetched, the dog has to be able to understand and comply with the word 'fetch,' both with and without pressure. Also, while force fetching involves a certain amount of pressure, it can be done without causing major stress for the dogs and doesn't

---

[2] Force fetch: A process of teaching the dog to hold the object it is retrieving without dropping it. The dog must also learn to hold the retrieve object properly, which means no chewing, chomping, or mouthing. If the dog does drop its retrieve object, the dog must be able to pick it up immediately and understand the correction given for dropping the object.

[3] Delivery to hand: Delivering the retrieved object to the handler's hand, without dropping it.

need to be the chamber of horrors that some people turn it into."

Jim led the black lab puppy out to the center of the barn. As he went to insert the bumper into the young lab's mouth, the pup wildly started swinging his head back and forth. When I had witnessed this previously, the trainer had yelled and forced the bumper into the dog's mouth out of anger and frustration. I winced from the memory.

But Jim was different. Poised and calm, he held the pup firmly by the collar until it relaxed. Again, Jim tried to put the bumper into the pup's mouth with the same result. This time, Jim pulled on the pup's collar while gently saying, "Sit," until the pup relaxed once again. This happened seven or eight times before Jim could even put the bumper into the pup's mouth.

Jim continued to teach the pup to hold for about twenty minutes. Several times, Jim had to give a slight jerk and shake as he held the pup's collar in order to get this wild little thing to become stable. He ended the session with a success. Even though the pup held the bumper for less than five seconds, he did it with some form of calmness and stability.

After the session, Jim threw a happy bumper for the pup.[4] I asked Jim why he did that when the pup did not seem to do all that well. He smiled and said, "These sessions are a bit stressful, and it's important to end with some fun. Though the pup was a bit on the wild side, he did make some effort, as well as some progress. We'll build on that."

I also asked him if he always did the exercise for about this length of time.

"Pretty close," he answered, "Give or take a few minutes, depending on what's going on. There are other things this pup needs to be learning right now, so I don't want to spend all my training time on one thing.

"Also, I like to sequence the training so the dogs don't get soured on it. I'd like him to look forward to the training the next day. Later, I'll get him in the water and throw some marks[5] for him. This will be a stress reliever, as well

---

[4] Happy bumper: A bumper thrown for the dog with no rules attached. It rewards the dog for a job well done and can also relax nervous dogs.

[5] Marks: Something the dog sees thrown that it's supposed to retrieve, or, in the case of hunting, something the dog sees fall. A good marking dog will watch the fall, go directly to the area of the fall, and, in a very short period of time, find the object and bring it back. Dogs vary in their marking ability. It is a highly sought after trait in hunt test and field trial dogs. Marking ability is obviously beneficial for hunting dogs as well.

as a productive part of his training. For now, though, let me get another young dog out and show you how the principle of leadership works when teaching the same task to a pup with a totally different temperament."

Jim then brought out a young female lab. She seemed happy but cautious; she wouldn't take her eyes off Jim.

"This is her second day doing force fetch," Jim explained. "Though the first day went well, she's a submissive dog who wants to do no wrong.

"Part of leadership is to train each dog in a way that best suits its temperament and in a way that not only produces the desired result but does so while cultivating a positive working attitude in the dog. This is our goal.

"Every dog is different, and some are very different. To train all dogs the same way, without taking these differences into consideration, is irresponsible dog training. Jack, there are dogs that get washed out or, worse yet, psychologically destroyed because of such negligence. Jack would you consider me a successful trainer if I produced some great dogs but in the process ruined other dogs?

"Of course not," I replied, though I think Jim wanted to make a point more than get an answer from me.

"Jack, it's critical that each of us be brutally honest with ourselves about how and what we are doing. Human nature is such that we are excellent at justifying our behavior. We find plenty of reasons for why it is okay to do what we do, and we can get so good at this that we begin to believe our own story.

"Furthermore, in many cases, we're not held accountable because no one knows truth of the matter but ourselves. The ruined dogs normally don't show up for the public to observe. If I ruin a dog, only I, and maybe the owner of the dog, would know. But while it's possible to hide the truth from others, we cannot hide it from ourselves. Eventually we all reap what we sow. Like I said, Jack – brutal honesty. In training, if the mindset isn't right, nothing else will be either."

I wrote furiously in my journal, trying to capture as much information as possible. As I looked back up, Jim had already inserted the bumper into the young lab's mouth. This dog responded differently from the previous dog. Apprehensive and almost motionless, she sat and held the bumper for a few seconds and then let it drop. Jim calmly picked up the bumper and inserted back into the pup's mouth, lightly tapping her under the chin as he said, "Hold." He praised her quietly, gently stroking the top of her head. This relaxed her immediately.

Jim paused between the hold commands and explained, "Notice how these two dogs are different, Jack.

The first needed a firmer approach, whereas this dog needs a firm approach but also lots of reassurance. Too much praise with the first dog would induce more unstable behavior, but praise soothes this dog. I purposely showed you two extremes so the contrast would be more obvious, but it's not always this clear cut." Jim continued with the young pup for ten more minutes or so and then ended with a few happy bumpers.

*****

As the week went on, Jim used different training situations to illustrate how leadership applied to dog training, and I continued to add to my journal. At this rate, I would soon need another notebook.

I spent most of Saturday evening going over my notes from the week. What an eye opener; there was more to this than I had realized. Though it was only the first week, I was beginning to see the importance of beginning with the proper training mindset.

As I reflected back on the week, I summarized the first principle of leadership.

# Principle One: Leadership

1. Leadership is having the dog's best interest and well-being as the top priority at all times, while producing results.
2. Ego has no place in leadership.
3. Leadership is based on trust and respect, not fear.
4. Leadership involves fair application of discipline. Failure to apply necessary discipline for fear that our dogs won't like us or for fear we are being "mean", is not leadership. Rather, such omission is detrimental to the dog/handler relationship.
5. Leadership is a presence, a state of mind. It can be cultivated.
6. Dogs need, even crave, true leadership
7. It is critical that the dog understand any pressure/discipline applied and how to stop or prevent it.
8. Strive to remain calm and poised during training. The dogs pick up on and respond to your demeanor.
9. How training is sequenced is critical to developing and maintaining a positive working attitude in the dog. Train each dog in a way that best suits its temperament, and in a way that produces the desired

result while cultivating a positive working attitude in the dog.

10. Be brutally honest with yourself. Don't be deceived into rationalizing and justifying improper training methods and philosophies. You will eventually reap what you sow.
11. Timing of praise is important. Praise may benefit one dog, while for another dog such praise may be unproductive.
12. Never forget that each dog is different and that different dogs need the training methods applied differently.

# CHAPTER FIVE

## *Principle Two: State of Mind – The Key to Responsible and Successful Training*

Jim was already in the barn waiting for me when I pulled into the Hill's driveway on Monday morning.

"Good morning, Jack." He glanced at the journal in my hand. "You're going to need that this week. We're doing things a little differently. We'll have our usual discussion, but then we'll head off to a local retriever club's training day to see this week's principle in action. Are you ready for our discussion on the second Principle, Jack?"

He waited while I reached for a pen.

"Great, let's get started. The second Principle is State of Mind. This is the key to responsible training."

"What do you mean by state of mind, Jim?" I asked curiously.

"Well, all the principles I am going to teach you are critical to successful dog training. But mastering this principle, Jack, is the biggest key to training responsibly. There are two components to training with the right state of mind." He raised two fingers in the air. "One, the state of mind you are in when you start training. And, two, the state of mind you allow yourself to get in based on how the training is going.

"Let's talk first about the state of mind you are in when you begin the training process. Jack, let's say you have had a rough morning, or a rough day for any number of reasons, and you're frustrated. Do you think that state of mind will affect how you train? How you respond to what the dog does?"

"Yes," I answered, "But I never really thought of how the state of mind I was in prior to training would affect training. Though, now that I think about it, it makes sense. It seems like any sort of disempowered state would affect your training, whether it be frustration, fatigue, crankiness, sadness, pain – even hunger."

"Exactly. But here's the catch, Jack. While people may know this on an intellectual level, they still fall into the trap of allowing their disempowered state to affect what they do and how they respond to their dogs. And once someone starts down that road, it's difficult to get out of it until it is too late.

"Though I won't get into a psychological discussion on how to change a disempowered state of mind, I will say that acute awareness of your state of being will help you avoid getting sucked into this abyss. Likewise, this awareness will allow you to catch yourself when you are reacting in an unproductive manner, so that you can change your behavior.

"But the bottom line is do whatever you can to start a training day or training session in the right state of mind. And if you find you've been hijacked and can't get yourself out of that disempowered state, then you would be better off not to train that day. No training is better than unproductive training."

"You want to train professionally, right Jack?" He didn't wait for an answer. "Well, professionals often feel pressured to stick to a schedule because clients are paying for training. But here's how I see it: if I were paying someone to train my dog, I would rather they miss a day of training than have an unproductive training session. I need to be able to trust a trainer with my dog's well-being."

I nodded my head in tacit agreement as I scribbled in my journal.

"The second state of mind, Jack, is the unproductive state that results from your reactions to the dog and the actual training. It comes from the meaning we attribute to difficulties, whether they occur in the past or in the moment. And it usually manifests in an unproductive cycle of making unfair corrections and failing to make legitimate corrections."

"Hmm...what do you mean?" I asked, a little puzzled.

Jim obligingly replied, "Let me give you a couple examples.

"Let's say you're at a hunt test, and your dog does something that causes him to fail but also embarrasses you. And it's normal to feel embarrassment – I mean who wants to look bad in front of their peers, right? So the next day, you take your dog out, and instead of working through the trouble spot with poise, you let your bruised ego run the show. You make some unfair corrections. Then, because you care about your dog, you start to feel guilty; to assuage your guilt, you fail to make legitimate corrections. You get emotional about something that your dog did in the past, and it just snowballs.

"Or take a different scenario," Jim continued, "You're out with your training group, and your dog is ignoring you. You get ticked off, even embarrassed, and you respond by making unproductive and unfair corrections. In other words, you allow difficulties in the present moment to put you in a state of mind where you behave in a way that you will later regret. Does that make sense?"

"I think so."

"Jack, it's imperative that we do all we can to begin training in a productive state of mind and to maintain a productive mindset during training. Also, it's never wise to correct out of emotion; that idea itself could be a stand-alone principle."

I could tell by the intensity and solemnness of his expression that he took this subject especially seriously.

"Jack," Jim reiterated, "No one ever gets it perfect; however, we must always do the best we can."

*****

The club had just started running dogs when we arrived at the training day. Jim introduced me to a few people, and then we grabbed a couple of chairs and sat down to watch.

We saw dog and handler teams at all different levels display some exceptional work, but then a dog and handler got into trouble when it came to delivering a bird to hand. As the dog came out of the pond, it dropped the bird at the water's edge. The handler told the dog to fetch it up. The young dog picked up the bird, took a few steps, and dropped it again.

"Fetch!" commanded the handler. This continued three or four more times, with the dog making no progress toward the handler. With each repeated command, the handler became more frustrated, and frustration escalated into anger.

The handler then charged toward the dog, grabbed its ear, and pulled its head down towards the bird while yelling "Fetch!" At this point, the dog froze in a state of uncertainty. The dog appeared to be on the soft side.[6] Confused and worried, the dog apprehensively picked up the bird but then immediately dropped it. The handler pinched the dog's ear even harder, but to no avail. At this point, the handler completely lost it. He shoved the bird into the dog's mouth and roughly cuffed the dog under the chin, yelling, "Hold! Hold! Hold!" The handler cuffed the dog under the chin again, put the leash back on, and angrily chastised the dog as he stalked off to his dog truck

"What happened there?" I asked Jim.

"Without knowing the history of the dog and it's level of training, it's hard to say exactly. But this I can tell you: as we just saw, anytime you allow your emotions to run rampant, nothing good can come out of it."

I nodded and remarked, "It appeared the dog did not fully understand the fetch command, and the madder the handler got, the more uncertain the young dog became."

"That's right, Jack," Jim replied. "A correction may have been appropriate in that situation if the dog truly

---

[6] Soft: Sensitive to pressure, correction, or even tone of voice. This type of dog can be difficult to train. However, they can turn out to be the best dogs if they have talent and are handled correctly.

understood the command. But the problem is that, even if a correction is warranted, if it is applied in the midst of negative emotions, the correction will not be fair, and possibly even detrimental to the dog's well-being and progress.

"Jack," said Jim, tempering his tone, "I know the handler a little, and I think he does have the dog's best interest at heart. In this particular case, he allowed the heat of the moment to cause him to lose it emotionally. You can see how this can happen to well-intentioned people and how emotional mastery is a critical factor in successful dog training."

Jim and I watched some more dogs work and then took a break for lunch. As we were eating our sandwiches, we overheard a handler talking about what had happened at the previous weekend's field trial. His dog had cheated the water[7] on the way to a retrieve, and apparently this had cost the team a ribbon. It seemed the handler had taken the dog's cheating the water personally. Even a week later, he got increasingly worked up about it as he spoke. This dog and handler team was to be the first to run after the

---

[7] Cheating the water: Failing to get in the water when the path to the retrieve is through the water. A dog can also cheat the water by not staying in the water for the proper distance on the way to a retrieve. Cheating the water can cause a dog to lose track of its mark.

lunch break, so I was especially curious to see what was going to happen.

The club had used a small, round pond to set up an advanced test – a water double[8] with a land blind.[9] The first retrieve was thrown into the middle of the pond, while the second retrieve was thrown for the dog to cut just the small left corner of the pond and not run around the water. The blind land retrieve was placed well past the water, with the line[10] about 30 yards off to the right of the pond.

When the first dog and handler walked up to the line, the handler looked determined to make the dog pay for embarrassing him the previous weekend. The dog picked up the first retrieve in the open water with no problem. The handler then sent the dog for the second retrieve – the one the dog was supposed to cut the corner of the pond and not run around. But sure enough, the dog went to run around the water. The handler stood ready. As the dog got

---

[8] Water double: Two retrieves through the water to be made one after the other. The last object retrieved is called the "memory bird."

[9] Land blind/water blind: A "blind retrieve" is a retrieve that the dog did not see fall. The idea is for the dog to have the faith to take a straight path to the bird. If the dog deviates, the handler stops the dog with a whistle and directs the dog to the bird by using hand signals.

[10] The line: The "line" can mean either the path to the retrieve or the place where the handler stands during the test.

around the edge of the pond, the handler, without warning, inflicted a huge, long correction with the electronic collar and yelled, "No! Here!" The dog yelped for several seconds and then tip-toed back to the handler.

The handler re-sent the dog, and this time the dog got in the water. However, the dog did not cut the corner at the angle that was desired; instead, it squared straight across the pond and made the retrieve. The handler looked rather smug as he commented to those watching how he had gotten the correction he was looking for.

The dog and handler "team" still had the blind retrieve to pick up. As the handler tried to get the dog lined up to send it for the blind, the dog acted nervous and anxious, "bugging" they called it. The handler got frustrated because he could not get the dog to look out towards the blind retrieve. Finally, he sent the dog, and the dog immediately headed for the water. The handler stopped the dog and gave it a hand signal away from the water, towards the blind. The dog refused that hand signal and, once more, went towards the water.

Again and again, the dog refused the hand signals. Finally, the handler exploded with anger and brutally corrected the dog. It got so ugly that someone had to step in to calm the handler down and recommend that he simplify the task so the dog could at least finish the retrieve. As they walked back to their truck, the dog looked frazzled, and a bewildered look replaced the handler's enraged expression. I'm not sure he even knew what had just happened.

I turned to Jim, who had a disgusted look on his face, and asked him what had happened.

"First of all, Jack, I want to say that the electronic collar, when used correctly and with the proper attitude and mindset, can be one of the most effective and fair ways to correct a dog. But what you just witnessed does not fall into that category. The handler went into the training session with a mindset of revenge, rather than truly trying to teach the dog a skill. And unfortunately this happens far too frequently."

Jim went on to explain, "Jack, what you saw is what I call 'protecting our ego.' As I've said before, people go to great measures to protect their egos and justify their behavior. And though a correction was in order, the mindset behind it was wrong. The correction was made out of emotion and a correction made out of emotion is never right, even when the correction is warranted. The handler's biggest mistake, however, was making the corrections on the blind retrieve."

"What do you mean?" I asked.

"Well, Jack, think back to the second retrieve. The handler severely corrected the dog for running around the pond. After that severe correction, the dog got in the water. Then when the handler tried to send the dog on the blind retrieve, the dog became anxious. Do you know why, Jack?"

I said I did not.

"Well Jack, if the handler had run the blind before the dog got corrected for trying to run around the water, it's unlikely the dog would have had a problem on the blind retrieve. Dogs can do the wrong things for the right reasons. Because of the correction for trying to run around the water, in the dog's mind it needed to get in the water. In other words, the dog's response was, 'I better seek water and seek it fast.' This is why the dog got nervous and buggy when the handler was trying to line the dog up away from the water and why the dog was refusing the hand signals. The problem was that the handler didn't recognize this and interpreted the refusal as disobedience. But the dog was actually trying to be good!

I was still a little confused. "But don't you usually correct a dog for refusing hand signals?" I asked.

"Yes, Jack, there are times a dog needs to be corrected for refusals. But during training, you must consider the dog's intention. I would never correct a dog for trying to do what it thought was the right thing – in other words, doing the wrong thing for the right reason. With certain types of dogs, the fallout from correcting a dog in this situation can be disastrous. If done often enough, this can destroy the dog's confidence, creating a vortex of other problems followed by more corrections. Jack, this is irresponsible dog training, even if the dogs can psychologically handle it."

Deeply focused, Jim paused for a moment and collected his thoughts.

"Jack, can you see how the principles integrate? Think back to the overarching principle of why the mindset behind dog training is more important than the methods. The wrong mindset is always the root cause of unfair and sometimes even abusive application of methods. If the mindset is right, mistakes in training and methods can much more easily be corrected, and there is no psychological damage done to the dogs, which, to me, is the where the real danger lies.

"Forgive me for going on a bit of a rant here, but I have seen many dogs ruined because of trainers training with an improper mindset, possibly dogs that could have become great dogs."

Everything Jim told me made perfect sense. Without his insights into training, it may have taken me awhile to come to the same conclusions, if ever.

"Jack, we've seen enough to make this week's lesson and principle very clear. Let's head back."

We said our goodbyes to the training group and headed back to the farm.

*****

On the drive back, Jim allowed me time to record the day's activities into my journal. That night, we rehashed the day's events over dinner. During the training sessions throughout the week, Jim pointed out the situations that can hijack your mindset and how to prevent it. He also gave anecdotes from his years of training and what he learned from them. While I gained understanding from Jim's insights throughout the week, it was the training day that had made a profound impression. I had witnessed first-hand the destructiveness of training with a disempowered state of mind, and I would never forget it.

As the week ended and I reviewed my journal, I noted the major ideas to remember.

## Principle Two: State of Mind - The Key to Responsible and Successful Dog Training

1. Training with the proper state of mind is the key to training responsibly.
2. The state of mind you bring to a training session affects how you train and how you respond to the dogs, even if that state of mind has nothing to do with dog training.
3. Emotional mastery is a critical factor in successful dog training. You need not be a slave to your emotions.
4. Do all you can to start the training day in a productive frame of mind.
5. Being aware of your mental state will help you avoid making mistakes you will later regret.
6. Missing a day of training is better than training in an unproductive state of mind. Training under such circumstances could cost you much more than the missed day.
7. Work on a problem area with poise. Prioritize the dog's well-being. Don't allow your bruised ego to run the show.

8. Dogs can do the wrong thing for the right reason. Try not to correct a dog for doing what it thinks is right, even though it's not.
9. Be careful of the meaning you give to the dog's failures or mistakes. Try not to take the dog's mistakes personally.
10. Make every effort to never correct out of emotion.
11. Don't allow guilt or regret to cause you to fail to make appropriate corrections.
12. Even a warranted correction can lead to negative short and long term side effects if done out of emotion. Eventually, it will prove costly.
13. Just because a dog can handle an inappropriate correction, that does not make it right.
14. The right methods with the wrong mindset will never turn out right.

# CHAPTER SIX

## *Principle Three: Confidence*

When I first started working with Jim, I was not sure how his "mindset principles" would really apply to dog training, but I now wondered how one could train without them. I had come to the conclusion that these principles truly were foundational for successful dog training, at least how I had now come to define success. The principles I had learned so far had transformed my way of perceiving dog training. And we had only gotten through two principles; we had four more to go!

I was also amazed at the amount of information I had written down, and I couldn't imagine trying to remember it all without having taken notes. Had I not captured Jim's teachings in my journal, I would have forgotten the details of what he said, and I might not have had such insights. I would now have Jim's lessons to refer to for years to come. My journal was priceless.

As I pulled up to the barn, it had started to rain lightly. The weather forecast called for rain in the morning and clearing by the afternoon. It was more of a drizzle than a real rain, and I enjoyed it. As I parked, I could see that many people from Jim's training group had arrived. His training group came out to train with Jim three times a week. Depending on the day, the group ranged from six to ten people - hunt test and field trial people, as well as a few hunters. I had grown to enjoy the group days. I learned a lot watching other people handle their dogs, people who were committed to training their dogs in a positive, productive way. The close-knit group rooted for one another amidst the friendly heckling and teasing. I had been involved on a limited level with some other training groups, but none of them were a tight-knit community like this one. I was happy to be part of it, even if for only a limited time.

As I walked into the barn, the aroma of hot Vermont coffee permeated the air. A cup of coffee had become my daily priority. As I poured myself a cup, the group members jovially mocked me for being a few minutes late, asking me if I was still on California time. After a few minutes of chatting, Jim said, “Let's get started!”

Jim had not told me what this week's lesson or principle would be, but he did say he was going to involve the group in the discussion period. He thought it would be helpful to get some feedback from them. In his wisdom, Jim had waited until the third week to involve the group in our discussion time so that I could get to know and become comfortable with the group members.

Eight of us had gathered in a semi-circle, some sitting on hay bales and some on their lawn chairs. Jim sat on a hay bale at the open end of the half circle. Though it was drizzly and bit chilly outside, in the barn a wood stove burned brightly and kept us warm.

"Principle number three is Confidence. Jack, as we move forward, you'll see just how much the principles are intertwined and are part of the recipe for successful dog training. We have tangentially addressed Confidence in the previous principles, but we are going to go into it a bit deeper this week.

"Confidence not only helps us to make better decisions during the training process, but the dogs respond much better when we are poised. So much of what we have discussed has been about cultivating a mindset that prioritizes treating the dogs fairly. But remember that people sometimes relinquish the leadership role to the dog, even if they do it unintentionally. Think of if this way Jack: confidence is a mindset of calmness, certainty, and strength. Uncertainty is not a part of confidence; it is not leadership. In the dog's mind, uncertainty is weakness."

"Confidence has a different energy and feel to it than does frustration, anger, or uncertainty, and the dogs are excellent at picking up on these emotions. It seems as if our emotional state goes right down the lead into the dog. If a handler lacks confidence, a bold, independent dog will usurp the leadership role and become almost uncontrollable. Likewise, the handler's uncertainty will magnify an insecure dog's tentativeness. Either way, this won't produce good results. Whether in training or at an event, our confidence plays a huge part in how the dog responds, not only to us but to the environment and situation at hand."

"Preparing ourselves and our dogs definitely cultivates confidence. However, the true foundation of confidence is believing that you are capable. You have to believe in yourself, and that starts with how you think and how you interpret things."

Jim took a sip of coffee and continued, "Some people get so stuck in the fear of failing that it's almost impossible to cultivate confidence. And when you fear failure, confidence evaporates. Let's face it: if you are competing at anything at a high level, you are going to have times when you fail, and maybe even fail in a big way. But you cannot let that control you.

"You can't have success without the possibility of failure, and if we could, success probably wouldn't mean much. Yet it is possibility of failure that makes success so sweet. So, yes, there will be disappointments. And even amidst the disappointments, you can enjoy the process by keeping the proper perspective. It's important to not lose sight of this point.

"I got off on a tangent here, Jack, but one of the hardest things I've had to do is get my clients to not be afraid of so-called 'failure.' If you're not afraid of it, the possibility of failure gives life flavor. This will go a long way in helping cultivate confidence. The bottom line is that it's almost impossible to perform above your level of confidence.

Jim paused, to let his lecture sink in, and after a moment one of the group members, Tess, spoke up.

"Jim, would you mind my sharing about my experience with Drake?"

"That would be wonderful," replied Jim.

Tess looked around at the group and began. "When I first started training with Jim, I was hesitant to discipline Drake. I worried about being unfair, so I erred on the side of permissiveness and allowed him walk all over me. Drake's a high drive lab, and when he went into retrieving mode, I had absolutely no control over him. I didn't think much of it at first because we'd had some success in the junior hunt tests. But I hadn't realized that the lower level successes had resulted only from his natural ability and his enthusiasm to retrieve. When we tried to move up to a higher level, everything fell apart because Drake didn't respect me.

"I had created such a long-standing pattern that changing Drake's behavior and perception of me proved difficult. Yet the most challenging task was building my confidence and convincing myself that I could be a leader. Between Drake and me, Jim certainly had his work cut out for him.

"Fortunately, Jim trains people as well as he trains dogs. He transformed me as a trainer and handler by changing my thinking. During the group training days, Jim coached me to be mindful of my emotions and to act opposite to my fear. Each time I noticed my uncertainty, I acted confident. This wasn't easy at first, and it didn't happen overnight. You may have heard the statement, 'Fake it until you make it.' Well that was me for a while. But as I gained proficiency at managing my emotions, I saw an incredible difference in my confidence. Of course, once Jim realized how confident I could be in training, he pushed me further and had me work on my confidence at events, which was a whole different ballgame.

"At events I usually became a nervous wreck in the holding blind.[11] Everyone has butterflies, but I would almost make myself sick. My nerves affected my decision-making when I handled Drake, and even worse, Drake would sense my anxiety through the leash and become even more out of control. I feared making bad decisions and looking foolish in front of other people. Again, Jim urged me to attend to my fears and act opposite, and soon Drake and I began to succeed at the higher levels.

"You see, Jack, all the great training methods in the world weren't going to help me until I became confident enough to lead. It may sound corny, but if I hadn't learned to believe in myself, Drake never would have respected me, and we never would have been able to run the more advanced hunt tests. We still have much to work on, but we're coming from a totally different place now."

I listened, astonished at Tess's story. I had watched her work with Drake over the past few weeks, and her confidence had impressed me. She was one of the better handlers in the group and carried herself with poise and composure. I never would have guessed that she had faced such challenges. When Tess finished her story, the

---

[11] Holding blind: An enclosure where the dog and handler stand while waiting for their turn to run. It is intended to obstruct the dog's view of the test.

whole group gave her a standing ovation. Jim remained standing as the others sat back down. He gazed proudly at Tess.

"Thank you for sharing, Tess. You and Drake have come such a long way. Bravo."

Jim then turned to me. "You see, Jack, the key to confidence is believing that you can achieve the goals you have set. Yes, for some people dog training comes more naturally than for others, yet I believe almost anyone can become what is necessary to achieve their dog training goals if they are totally committed. But you have to put fear of failure aside. You have to believe it, really commit to it, and then go for it.

"One last thing I want to touch on before we wrap up our discussion and head out training is the difference between confidence and arrogance. Confidence is not about having an attitude of 'look at me and how great I am,' and spouting off to anyone who will listen about all you have done and all you are going to do. A truly confident person feels no need to babble on about such things. Such talk is a symptom of insecurity and often offends more people than it impresses. Jack, true confidence neither fears failure nor needs to constantly prove itself.

"Now, enough talk, let's go training and actually put these principles into action."

With that the group headed out to another fantastic day of training.

*****

That week, we had a few days of wet weather but nothing to affect training all that much. Fall in Vermont was a wonderful time to learn the principles of dog training. After our discussion at the beginning of the week, I really paid attention to how the presence or absence of confidence affected the dog's performances. Growing up playing sports and being highly competitive, I could relate to much of what Jim had said.

At the end the week, Jim and Cindy invited me to dinner at the farm. I appreciated the opportunity to spend time with them in a non-dog training environment, and I tried to keep the talk about dog training to a minimum because I didn't want to be rude to Cindy. However, I did make it clear to both of them how much I appreciated their hospitality and Jim's agreeing to mentor me. I told Jim how I had already learned much more than I ever expected and how fortunate I was to be given this opportunity. This inner game of dog training was not only fascinating but also incredibly effective. Developing a close friendship with Jim and Cindy made the process that much more enjoyable. I had become quite attached to Jim and Cindy Hill.

*****

Back at my hotel, I to reviewed my week and summarized the major points in my journal.

# Principle Three: Confidence

1. Being confident will help you make better decisions
2. Dogs sense if a person is confident or not. This greatly determines how dogs respond to you.
3. Dogs need and even crave leadership.
4. Uncertainty is not leadership and is actually detrimental to dog training.
5. You have to believe you can be the leader.
6. It is almost impossible to perform above your level of confidence.
7. Being truly confident will make you a better leader, trainer and handler.
8. How you think and see yourself has a big part to do with how confident you are.
9. Being properly prepared cultivates confidence.
10. There is a difference between being confident in training verse at an event.
11. Believe that you are capable of being a good trainer and handler and achieving your dog training goals.
12. Don't fear failure. Without the possibility of failure, success wouldn't mean much.
13. Confidence and arrogance are different things.

# CHAPTER SEVEN

## *Principle Number Four: Productivity*

Jim was working one of the dogs when I pulled up to the training barn. "Perfect timing. I'll put this dog away and then meet you in the barn at our usual conversation spot."

While I waited for Jim, I poured some coffee for us both and settled into my usual spot in our rustic conference area.

"Ooh, thank you," said Jim, as I motioned towards his coffee cup when he walked in. "Jack, I want to give you a little background before I jump into this week's principle. My mentor taught me that a great trainer is one that can get the best out of every dog, not just the talented ones. In other words, almost anyone can produce good results with a talented dog, but a great trainer can get results even with a mediocre dog.

"You see, Jack, great trainers can get fantastic results from ordinary dogs because they train on the right things, use appropriate methods, read the dogs correctly, and adjust to what they see. They know what to train on, which means knowing what they are training for – the rules of the game, so to speak. And they consistently focus their training on these things.

"On the other hand, Jack, many well-intentioned people put a lot of time into training and don't achieve the results they desire in a reasonable amount of time. In extreme cases, they put all that time in and actually have the dog further from achieving their goals than when they started. Jack, it would be an absolute shame to put in hours and hours of training and not have the dog much closer to your goals, or for it to take twice as long as it should.

"I think everyone would agree that it takes time and hard work – or hard play depending on how you look at it – to train a stellar retriever. I refer to this as 'activity.' But activity is insufficient. What we're striving for is productivity. That's this week's principle. To train productively, we must first make sure we are training on the right things and, second, use appropriate methods with a proper mindset."

Jim paused, waiting for me to finish writing in my journal.

"A common mistake I see, Jack, is training on things that don't properly prepare the dog for the goals they want to achieve, or at least prepare them in a way that gives the dog the best chance to succeed.

"Successful dog training is about preparing the dogs for what they are going to commonly encounter in whatever sport the dog is involved in. You wouldn't spend your time training an agility dog on retriever work, or a cattle dog on agility work. You would specify your training based on what you were going to do with the dog.

"For example, if someone is training hunting dogs the same way as they would for a field trial or hunt test dog, the results will likely be less than ideal.[12] Though the basics are the same for these dogs regardless of the sport played, what a hunting dog needs to see and be exposed to is very different from what a field trial or hunt test dog needs to be exposed to and trained on. A hunting dog has no real need to be exposed to having gunners[13] and handlers in white coats.[14] This is not to imply Jack that a hunting dog cannot be a good field trial dog or field trial dog a good hunting dog. Many people are successful at doing both. The point is if a hunting dog will never see a

---

[12] Hunt tests and field trials versus hunting: The skills a dog needs to succeed at hunting, hunt tests, or field trials differ greatly depending on the dog's specialty. The fundamentals are the same, but after that, the training varies.

[13] Gunners: People out in the field who throw marks for the dogs. This term is used in hunt tests and field trials. "Gunners" can also be shooters; the people shooting the birds.

[14] White coats: Gunners wear white coats in field trails but not in hunt tests. Because the retrieves are so long in filed trials, the white coats help the dogs locate the gunners.

field trial, it would be a waste of time to have the same training program as a field trial dog.

"Jack, if you took the best hunting dog there is, that dog could still not compete in a field trial. Not because the field trial game is better, but because the things the field trial dogs are asked to do are different. As result, they must be trained differently. As you have seen during our training days, we train on different things with different dogs. Our hunting dogs don't need to do a water blind where it swims along a shoreline for 100 yards or more. Though a hunt test and field trial dog would need this skill, it would be almost useless if I spent training time mastering a skill that a hunting dog would never need to do. This is a rather obvious example Jack, but there are other situations where the differences are more subtle but no less important."

I looked up from my journal and waited for Jim to continue.

"The next part of the productivity principle is appropriately applying methods with the proper mindset. The proper application of methods, which has a lot to do with our attitude, plays a big part in the proper use of time and productivity.

"Do you see the overlap between the previous principles, Jack? This goes back to our main premise that mindset is more important than methods. Some trainers would achieve great results by using almost any method, while others would get terrible results no matter which method was used. But the bottom line is that the right methods applied to things that don't prepare the dog for the goals we have won't produce the best results possible. And, depending on the talent level of the dog, may produce poor results.

"Jack, my mentor also taught me the corollary of how people can take too much credit for the success of a talented dog; they mistakenly think it is their training that made the dog great. You see, talented dogs can make up for bad training. My mentor told me to remember that I am not as good a trainer as the talented dogs make me look, nor am I as bad a trainer as the not-so-talented dogs make me look.

"As we are training this week, Jack, you'll see how all this works in the training process. Now that you are aware of this principle I think you will more fully understand why we do what we do in the training process. So let's get training."

*****

During the week, I once again realized the importance of awareness when it comes to successful training. As I observed the training with a fresh outlook on the principle of productivity, I began to realize how haphazardly I had trained in the past. With my newly found awareness, I began to see how the proper use of my training time could make a huge difference in the achievement of my dog training goals. As I went through my weekly review of my notes in my journal, I fully realized the vast difference between activity and productivity.

# Principle Four: Productivity

1. Activity and time is a vital part of training, but it does not produce results in and of itself.
2. Activity is not the same thing as productivity.
3. Successful training comes from training on the right things with the proper mindset. Prepare the dogs for what they will commonly encounter.
4. A reminder: Mindset is more important than methods.
5. Proper application of methods plays a big part in the productive use of time.
6. Practice does not make perfect: perfect practice makes perfect. It is possible to spend a lot of time training and actually make the dog less likely to be successful.
7. Producing great results with a talented dog does not necessarily make me a great trainer.
8. A great trainer gets the best out of each dog he trains.

# CHAPTER EIGHT

## *Principle Five: The Compound Effect*

It was hard to believe that I was starting my fifth week of what had become an incredible dog training odyssey. I was excited for what lay in store for me this week, but I was also beginning to feel pangs of disappointment as I realized how soon my journey would end. I would only have one week left after this week, and it seemed like just yesterday that I had nervously pulled into the Hill's driveway to start this process.

I was thankful that Jim had given me the journal. Each time I reviewed my notes, I gained a deeper understanding of the Principles. Jim had revolutionized my conceptualization of dog training. At times I felt a bit overwhelmed, but I knew I had grasped the meaning behind the principles and just needed to gain experience putting them into practice.

When I pulled up to the barn, I could see Jim sitting on one of the hay bales, drinking a cup of coffee. As I poured myself a cup, I noticed Jim had a sly grin on his face.

"Jack, I have a question for you: if you were given a choice between taking $3 million in cash this very instant or a single penny that doubles in value every day for thirty-one days, which would you choose?"

I was expecting a question related to dog training, but without hesitation, I answered, "The three mil, of course."

"Well Jack you may regret that choice if you actually had the chance to make it," Jim chided me.

"Regret it?" I said, "How in the world would I regret the three mil?"

"Well, Jack, the choice that would lead to greater wealth is the penny doubling every day for thirty-one days."

"You've got to be kidding me!" I responded, not totally buying his answer.

"Jack, do you know what the total amount of the penny doubled after ten days would be?"

"Not off the top of my head."

"Well, Jack, the amount would be $5.12. But at the end of the thirty-one days the total would be $10,737,418.24."

"No way!" I responded.

"Do the math, Jack. It's the truth."

Totally astonished, I asked, "So how does this relate to dog training?"

"Jack, the point of the doubling penny analogy is to show the importance of the effect seemingly small, consistent actions, taken over a period of time have on not only wealth accumulation, but every area of life, including dog training.

"Success in dog training does not come from one quantum leap; it comes from a series of consistent right actions with a proper mindset as the foundation. This is what I call the Compound Effect. When compounded over a period of time, what may seem inconsequential today can produce massive results. But also realize the flip side of the coin: consistent wrong actions, which may also seem inconsequential, can produce massive unproductive results.

"Jack, consistent action taken daily or almost daily is much better and more productive than massive time and action taken inconsistently. Training for twenty to thirty minutes a day on the right things with the proper mindset is much more productive than training for two hours twice a week."

"But what if someone training their own dog only has the weekends to train?" I asked.

"I will say this, Jack, I realize how hard it may be for people to train five to six days a week. And if all someone can do is train on the weekends, then they will have to make the very best of that situation. Even though it isn't ideal, there are people that get pretty good results from doing so. But the danger is in trying to stuff too much information into a training session. Dogs can only absorb so much information at one time. If you do too much without allowing the information to be absorbed, the dog won't be able to apply the information as well as they could in smaller doses. And in some cases, too much training in a short period of time can actually be detrimental."

"I can totally relate to that," I said to Jim. "I know I learn much better by taking in little pieces of information over time rather than being bombarded with an overwhelming amount of information all at once. And I guess that's why they say it's better to exercise a little each day than three hours twice a week." I immediately felt embarrassed – I wasn't sure what that had to do with dog training – but Jim smiled.

"Something like that, Jack."

Suddenly, I thought of Jim's puppy, Fenway. A devoted Boston Red Sox fan, Jim already had Fenny doing things better than many hunting dogs I had been around, including a couple of mine. Fenny could deliver to hand, do some simple doubles, and even take hand signals. I had never seen a puppy doing such things; in fact I didn't even realize it was possible.

During the short time I had been here, I had seen Fenny make incredible strides in her training. Jim had worked her briefly throughout our training days, and as I looked back, it was a perfect example of the Compound Effect. Taken in daily doses, none of the things Jim had been doing with her looked that amazing at the time; yet where she was now compared to when I first arrived was remarkable.

When I shared my thoughts on Fenny's progress, Jim agreed it was a good example.

"Jack," Jim asked me, "You know how you've commented how it's incredible what the dogs can do?"

"Yes," I replied, "I'm still amazed at the things I've seen the dogs do."

"Well, Jack, what these dogs can do is amazing, especially when you see the dogs doing the advanced work. It almost looks miraculous to the casual observer. But when you go through the whole process step by step, day by day, the result, though still amazing, doesn't seem quite as incredible. By the time you get to the advanced stage, you see it as a natural result. This isn't to say that a person doesn't experience "wow" moments during the process, but it's not miraculous.

"This phenomenon exists in everything from playing sports to playing a musical instrument. What many call 'genius' is really the result of consistent, right actions and a lot of hard work over an extended period of time. I'm not trying to take anything away from the great things these dogs do, Jack. The point is that these incredible results aren't an overnight success but rather a result of consistent, correct actions – what I call the Compound Effect. Jack, there can be great breakthroughs in a day, but again, these are almost always the result of the work put in to get to the breakthrough.

"On the other hand, Jack, the Compound Effect can work against you. Problems that seem to crop up overnight are often the negative results of the Compound Effect. For example, many well-intentioned clients have told me that they did not want to mess up their new puppy before formal training began, so they didn't do anything. This actually sets the Compound Effect into motion in a negative direction. After a few months of "doing nothing," this cute, cuddly puppy is likely a living terror! Another example is when we fall into bad habits and allow certain things to become so automatic that, by the time we recognize the problem, it's difficult to fix.

"However, one of the biggest mistakes I see, Jack, is when people treat training and events as the same thing. Our goal at an event is to make the dog look great and avoid any problems that would alert a judge to the dog's weaknesses. Contrarily, the purpose of training isn't to have the dog look good and avoid problems but rather to improve the dog. If we avoid the dog's weaknesses and just get by without mastering the necessary skills, we aren't making the dog better. And if we do this often enough, the Compound Effect will come back to bite us. You see, Jack, the Compound Effect is always at work in one direction or the other, and to one degree or another. Now, you have more leeway with a talented dog, but don't ever allow a talented dog to allow you to settle for mediocrity. Does this all make sense?"

"Yes, it does," I answered. "I have often seen people trying to get through a training setup instead of trying to get something from the training setup, though at the time I did not know the difference."

"Well put," replied Jim, with a pleased tone in his voice. "Now what do you say we go out and put this principle into action."

*****

By the end of the week of training, I had a totally different perception of the purpose of training and the vital importance of consistent right actions. As I reviewed my notes for the week I summarized them as follows.

## Principle Five: The Compound Effect

1. Little things add up to big things, in one direction or the other.
2. Small, consistent, and correct actions are what cause great results. Success rarely comes from one quantum leap.
3. What seems inconsequential today can have massive consequences in the future.
4. Dogs can only absorb so much information at one time. Perhaps this goes for people as well.
5. Though rarely impressive in the moment, the "little things" can prove very impressive in the long term.
6. Doing nothing is using the Compound Effect in a negative direction.
7. Be aware of the Compounding bad habits that creep into your training.
8. The purpose of training is to make the dog better, not to avoid problems.
9. Don't try to just get through training. Get from training.
10. Sacrificing high standards today will prove painful later.
11. Don't ever settle for mediocrity.

# CHAPTER NINE

## *Principle Six: Equilibrium*

I felt a mixture of emotions going into my final week of training with Jim. I would miss the mentorship, the positive training environment, and the friendships I had cultivated. Yet I was also enthusiastic about putting all I had learned into my own personal training program. I had a new puppy on the way, and I was eager to get started with her. At any rate, I felt even more determined to make every minute of my final week count.

As I drove up to the barn, I could see Jim doing a drill with Fenny in the yard. Jim threw her a happy bumper and greeted me with a big smile.

"Well, Jack, this is your last week, and I'm sure it's as bittersweet for you as it is for me. To give you a proper send-off, we're having a barbecue with the whole gang on Sunday. Also, Cindy and I would love to have you over for brunch on Sunday. This way we can have a final discussion that integrates what you've learned over the six weeks you've been here."

"I don't know what to say. That all sounds great. Thank you," I sputtered, slightly overcome with emotion.

"So, let's get started, Jack. We've been building up to the sixth and final principle: Equilibrium. I'm sure you're aware of the definition of 'equilibrium,' Jack, but I will share my own with you. I think of equilibrium as balance – the balance between success and failure, praise and discipline, independence and dependence, ease and challenge. Any of these taken out of balance will not produce the best results and may even produce disastrous results in some cases. And when I say 'balance,' Jack, I mean a balance that produces the best attitude possible in the dog with the best results.

"Each dog's point of equilibrium will be different because each dog differs in ability and temperament and must be trained according to its unique personality. Take a confident, independent dog with incredible drive, a 'fire breather' as some call them. This type of dog can experience more failure than a less driven, softer dog that is more of a team player. When I say 'failure,' I mean instances where the dog needs help or a correction to complete the task. The hard-driving, independent dog can fail more often without negatively affecting its attitude and momentum. Actually, such failure reminds the hard-charging, 'it's all about me' type of dog that this is a team effort and that we are the captain of the ship. On the other hand, the soft, 'I want to please you, just show me what to do' type of dog needs a lot of success so it will actually gain more independence."

"So," I said, "We're trying to get one dog to be more dependent, more of a team player and we're trying to get the other dog to be more independent and comfortable making its own choices."

"Exactly," Jim replied. "You see, the same methods may be used but applied in different ways. Some experienced trainers do this intuitively; but the typical training books and videos that the average person learns from never discuss this point. The majority of the people I have come across don't give much thought to the dog's equilibrium. They dive into a training program without much thought to what the dog needs in order to keep the proper balance of success and failure, praise and discipline, independence and dependence.

"So how do you know when a dog isn't in balance?" I asked.

"Maintaining a dog's equilibrium is a challenge," answered Jim. "It has a dynamic nature. The dogs communicate when they are out of balance, and it's our job to read that properly. It's the same way a good coach knows the difference between when a player needs an attitude adjustment, to be brought back down to earth and humbled a bit, and when a player need a pep talk, needs to be built up and given some confidence. Athletes can crash and burn because they get too cocky, but athletes lacking in confidence, afraid to make a mistake also crash and burn. It's no different for dogs, trainers, and handlers."

"Hmm," I said, a little daunted. "It seems like a difficult thing to master."

Jim responded, "It is a difficult thing to master. That's part of the art of dog training. But it's not so much about mastery as it is about the pursuit of mastery. Simple awareness of this principle will make a huge difference in a training program. As with all the principles, awareness leads to proper mindset, which allows us to apply the methods in a more productive and responsible manner.

"Now that brings me to my next point, Jack. 'Responsible' is an important word. It's easy to get so caught up in results, ribbons, and performance that we forget the reasons why we got into dog training in the first place. I know that some people get into the different dog sports solely for the ribbons, solely for the performance, without much of a concern for the dog's well being. I've also heard people claim they have the dog's well-being in mind, but they don't act that way when the dog doesn't perform up to expectations. And I've seen people whose self-esteem is so tied to the dog's performance that they are just not capable of training responsibly. All of this is irresponsible, Jack, and it's tragic for the dog.

Jim paused for a moment and glanced towards the kennels.

"Jack, you eventually want to train dogs professionally. Know that we professionals can be the most susceptible to these failings. It becomes easier to rationalize irresponsible training when your livelihood depends upon it. I realized this danger early in my training career and vowed to set up my finances and my business so that I would not fall victim to this. It was one of the best things I ever did, Jack. There is a big difference between working and training because you want to, versus working and training because you have to."

Jim solemnly held my gaze. I knew better than to answer him with words. I just stared back, knowing that he could read me like he read his dogs.

*****

When I sat down to write in my journal at the end of the week, I realized that I was leaving in just a few days and that the twinge of sadness I had felt earlier in the week had grown into a sharp pang. However, my spirits lifted when I reminded myself that I still had the barbecue and Jim's going away talk to look forward to before I left.

# Principle Six: Equilibrium

1. Equilibrium is the balance between success and failure, praise and discipline, independence and dependence, ease and challenge.
2. Each dog will have its own point of equilibrium.
3. Each dog is unique and should be treated as such.
4. Successful training is about finding the proper balance.
5. Confidence is critical, but over confidence can be as much as a problem as a lack of confidence.
6. The art of dog training is finding that fine line between confidence and over confidence.
7. Just the awareness of cultivating the proper balance will make a huge difference in training. Strive to stay aware.
8. It is easy to get so caught up with the results and ribbons that you forget why you got into training in the first place.
9. Be a responsible dog trainer.
10. Be careful about rationalizing the way you train.

# CHAPTER TEN

## *One Last Thing: Be Careful of What You Become in Pursuit of What You Want*

Still tired from the barbeque the night before, I pulled into the Hill's circular drive one last time. I reached into my duffel bag and fumbled around for my journal, which was now so full of training ideas and insights that I wondered if I could remember them well enough to apply them consistently. Journal in hand, I once again climbed the porch steps and paused to take in all the sights and sounds.

"One day I will have a place like this," I murmured to myself.

Before I could knock, Cindy opened the door and gave me a warm hug. "I hope you're hungry!" she said.

Jim greeted me from the kitchen. He glanced at Cindy and then smiled wryly at me. "I'm glad you're here. Now I can get a reprieve from kitchen duty."

"Reprieve granted," quipped Cindy as she shook her head and smiled.

Within a few minutes we were seated at the dining table, enjoying another one of Cindy's great meals. Though not heavily involved in the actual training of the dogs, Cindy was an invaluable asset to Jim and a huge part of the success he had experienced. They were indeed a great team. For the next couple hours, the three of us joked and laughed and reminisced about my time there.

At some point Jim said, "Well Jack, as you know I didn't just have you over merely to reminisce and say goodbye. I wanted to have one more discussion that places everything else we've discussed into proper perspective. I've actually touched on it throughout the whole process, but I wanted to explicitly address it now."

As I glanced over at Cindy, she nodded and smiled as if to say, "This topic is of vital importance."

Jim rose from the table and said, "Lets go into my study."

I stood up, thanked Cindy for the lovely meal, and grabbed my journal for what I knew was going to be an interesting discussion.

*****

Jim's beautifully decorated study had a comfortable, intellectual feel. Jim sat down in what he called his 'reading chair,' an elegant, well-worn, mahogany leather chair. I took a seat on the matching leather couch across from

Jim. I had been inside the Hill home many times, but I had only glanced at his study. As I sat down, I thought to myself, "Now here is a place I could spend some time." Wall to wall, floor to ceiling bookcases filled two of the walls in the massive room. Other than in the public library, I had never seen so many books.

"May I look at your books?" I asked Jim.

"Certainly."

There were books on philosophy, religion, psychology, leadership, management, finances, human behavior, and, of course, dog training.

"Have you read all of these books?" I asked.

Jim chuckled. "I've read most of them, some more than once. I've yet to read them all, but just their presence makes me feel smarter."

"You've got such a wide range of books," I commented. "And there's no light reading on your shelves."

Jim smiled again. "Yeah, Cindy has often said she's never seen me read a book that didn't require some deep thinking."

"Well," I said with a grin, "I also feel smarter just being in here. This is a great room, Jim."

"Thanks, Jack. I spend much of my free time in here, studying and thinking. Now what do you say we get to our discussion?"

*****

"Jack," Jim began, "In whatever your endeavors may be, whether dog training or anything else you pursue in life, this last premise should always be your guiding principle. If you make it a priority and constantly stay aware of it, you will experience true success, as well as peace of mind."

I had never seen Jim quite this serious, so I knew what he was about to share with me was critically important.

"Jack, my philosophy has the dog's well-being at its core. As we've discussed, it's easy to get so caught up in the results we want, whether that be ribbons, trophies, or impressing others, that we end up doing things to our dogs that we would never have dreamed of when we started our dog training journey. This, in and of itself, is a shame. But a bigger shame is how adept people become at rationalizing their actions. When it gets to the point where you are rationalizing, you're in trouble. And the unfortunate thing is that once most people get to this point, they're in total denial of what's happening.

"Jack," Jim asked, "When we first met, I asked you about whether you would use questionable methods to win a National Championship if that was the only way to win. Now let's take that one step further: would it be worth it to win but in the process become someone you didn't want to become –to become someone your dog feared and mistrusted?"

Before I could reply, Jim continued on.

"Most people would answer 'No.' But you may be surprised at the percentage of people who answer 'No' but whose actions ultimately say 'Yes.' I've seen it time and again. People start out sincerely wanting what's best for their dog and appreciating the training process. They want their dogs to become the best they can be, and of course, to achieve some great results. Yet at some point, people's priorities get turned around, and the results end up taking precedence. A tree is known by its fruit, Jack, not by what kind of a tree it says it is or wants to be. And this is a very easy trap to fall into, especially once you have tasted some success."

I must have had a worried expression on my face because Jim quickly continued his explanation.

"Jack, I want to make it eminently clear that this isn't about judging people or stone throwing. This is about awareness, mine included; I am not immune to falling into this trap. I constantly have to evaluate my thoughts and actions. I've made many mistakes and probably still make more than I should. But I can honestly say that not a day goes by that I don't consciously evaluate my methods and motives.

"So how do you do it? You're a competitive person," I ventured. "I mean, you must be – you've won multiple National Championships."

"Yes, fiercely competitive," replied Jim. "I've spent most of my life playing sports. I'm not indifferent to results or achievements; I just place them in perspective. Sports have taught me that competition is just as much about improvement and realizing your potential as it is about winning and achievement. You see, Jack, winning isn't everything, but preparing to win is. You have to give every training day all you have and then let the results be what they may. We can't control the results, but we can control how we prepare."

"So do you view your drive and competitiveness as an asset?" I asked, trying to wrap my head around this concept.

"Absolutely. In fact, you likely won't achieve success in this sport if you don't have a burning desire and determination. Somebody who is nonchalant about preparing to win will never be truly successful, even if they happen to win. As for people who have a lackadaisical attitude about results, well that's often founded in lack of confidence. Whether or not they're conscious of it, people who don't believe in their abilities use this attitude to protect themselves from disappointment and failure."

"That makes sense," I said.

"I should warn you, Jack, that as you begin to apply these principles with your new puppy, especially once formal training begins, you probably won't get immediate results. People who lack understanding may snicker and mock your training. But you must not let this deter you. If you stay true to your philosophy, you will succeed in the end, and your success will last longer than the fleeting feeling a ribbon may bring. And the good news is you don't have to sacrifice one for the other. You can achieve both inner and outer success, and that is what true success really is."

Jim stood up, and I followed suit. He looked me straight in the eye.

"Jack, I believe you have what it takes to succeed in all you choose to do. I hope what I have taught you will help in all your pursuits, and I am grateful for the opportunity to have shared these principles with you. I wish you the best, and I hope you stay in contact. I'll be watching your progress with great interest."

I reached out to shake Jim's outstretched hand.

"Jim," I told him, "I don't have words to fully express what your mentorship has meant to me. All I can say is, 'Thank you.' You have forever changed the way I see the world. Know that I'll always do my best to follow the principles you've shared with me."

It was an emotional moment, one I will never forget.

*****

Driving away from the Hill Farm, I felt empty inside. Even though I knew we would stay in contact, I would deeply miss Jim. He had become so much more than a mentor. The sadness would stay with me for awhile, but as I boarded the plane for home, I thought of the puppy who would soon become part of my family. I felt the spark of inspiration that would fuel the next phase of my dog training journey.

# Conclusion

Now that I have finished writing this book, it is even clearer to me that I needed to write it for myself, as well as for others. I may never master all of these principles, but I commit to do so daily with all my heart and soul. My mistakes have been many, but with practice and reflection, they have become far less frequent. I hope that this book inspires readers to train their dogs in a manner that produces results and has the dog's best interest and well-being at the forefront.

I would also like to acknowledge my grandfather Jack Hayre, to whom this book is dedicated, for being the best mentor a boy, and then a man, could have. Without his guidance and inspiration, my life would have taken a much different path. This book would never have been written, and I would never have tasted true and lasting success. His example and teachings have much to do with any success I have achieved. For this, I will be eternally grateful. So once again Grampa, thank you!

For further information regarding Dennis Hayre,
his training videos, and other products and services,
go to DennisHayreKennels.com

CPSIA information can be obtained at www.ICGtesting.com
Printed in the USA
BVOW01s1632140813

328467BV00008B/263/P